World-Class Customer Service:

You Make a Difference!

7 Steps to Service
They'll Remember

JAMES R. BALL
JENNIFER A. KUCHTA

KEEP IT SIMPLE FOR SUCCESS™

World-Class Customer Service:
You Make a Difference!
7 Steps to Service They'll Remember

ISBN: 1-887570-10-1

Published in the United States by The Goals Institute.
Printed in the United States.

Keep It Simple for Success™
is a registered trademark of The Goals Institute.

For information please contact or visit us at:

The Goals Institute
P.O. Box 3736
Reston, VA 20195-1736
703·264·2000

www.goalsinstitute.com
www.kissbooks.com
Email: info@goalsinstitute.com

Dedications

Jim:

This book is dedicated with
love to my father and mother,
Mont and Beatrice Ball.

Jennifer:

This book is dedicated with
love to my father and mother,
Joseph and Theresa Kuchta.

Thanks and Appreciation

We want to thank the following individuals for their help.

Thanks to Jennifer Ball-Zinck, Mike Damitz, and Mike Hicks for your valuable input.

Special thanks to Carol Weaver for your valuable input and your great insights and ideas.

Thanks to Julie Young for your graphics support on the cover.

Thanks to Ann Hunter for your editorial input and help in polishing our words and the messages they carry.

Welcome

HELLO!

We want to welcome you on behalf of our *Keep It Simple for Success*™ team at The Goals Institute.

Congratulations! This book, *World-Class Customer Service: You Make A Difference!* is a ready reference and guide to help you be successful and grow in your career. It will make a difference.

Because you have this little book in your hands, we know that you want to do your best in serving your customers. To make reading it as personal to you as possible, we are going to call your customers and company "our customers" and "our company." We hope that you will think of us as part of your team.

If you have any questions or comments, please drop us a note or send us an email.

If you would like additional information about our other *Keep It Simple for Success*™ books or our keynotes and seminars, please visit us at www.kissbooks.com.

Best wishes for great service!

James R. Ball   Jennifer A. Kuchta

Contents

Contents

World-Class Customer Service:

You Make a Difference!

MAKE NO MISTAKE about your personal importance and the importance of your roles and responsibilities. *You* make a difference!

You are important

The fact that you are an associate of our company is significant. We hired you because you are needed to help us build our organization. Our business exists for one reason and one reason only. It is to find, serve, satisfy, and keep our customers.

So, when you think about it, everyone who works here is on our customer service team. That includes you.

We need you.

We are relying on you to do your job and fulfill your responsibilities.

Our success depends on how you do your part in serving our customers and making them glad they are doing business with us.

Our customers need you. They rely on you to help them meet their needs through the products and services we provide.

True, you are just one individual. However, you are one individual who is an essential and important link in our customer service chain.

You make a difference!

It is not unusual for someone like you to wonder whether you can make a difference or have an impact in a company such as ours.

"Why should I bother?" you may say to yourself.

You may ponder questions such as these: "Am I important?" "Does my part count?" "Does it really matter what I do or don't do?"

The answer to each of these questions is a resounding YES!

Yes, you are important. Yes, your part counts. Yes, it matters what you do and do not do.

Not only *can* you make a difference, we *expect* you to make a difference.

You affect how others feel about our company

You may be the one who helps a customer in such a special way that the customer tells ten of his or her friends about the remarkable service that you provided. Those ten friends may tell ten of their friends and each of those individuals may tell ten others. Before you know it, hundreds, and perhaps thousands of individuals will think better of our company and our services—all because of you and the extra care you took with one customer when it was needed.

Perhaps you think that it is an exaggeration to believe that you can directly affect how hundreds or thousands of people feel about our company. It is not.

What you say and do will be noticed. It will matter. Our customers will talk about it with each other.

You *are* our company

Never overlook the fact that you *are* our company—not just figuratively, but literally. You, along with all of our other associates, comprise our company.

Now that you are employed here, at work and even on your days off, you will be associated with our company by your friends, family members, and others. These individuals and the people they meet are our customers or potential customers.

Therefore, no matter where you go or what you do you have continual opportunities to affect how others view our company.

Because of this association, it is essential that you always act in a professional and appropriate manner that reflects the pride we all have in our organization.

Don't ever underestimate your importance in serving our customers. You do make a difference!

World-Class Service and You

OUR COMPANY NEEDS YOUR HELP. Our goal is to provide *World-Class Service* that attracts, delights, and retains an ever-growing base of loyal, satisfied customers.

To achieve this goal, everyone in our organization must do his or her part. That includes you.

What is *World-Class Service*?

World-Class Service means "the highest class of customer service in the world."

In other words, *World-Class Service* is the best there is. No better service on earth. None.

And not only must we be the best, we must be the best on a consistent basis, day-in and day-out.

When you think about it, *World-Class Service* on a consistent basis is an ambitious and extraordinary goal.

However, this goal is possible to accomplish and we are committed to its realization. With your help we can achieve it.

What's in it for you?

Why should you make the effort to provide *World-Class Service* for our customers?

There are many reasons you should make the effort, but two stand out.

First, you are an integral member of our Customer Service Team. It is your responsibility and obligation to help us achieve our goal. We are all counting on you to do your part. You will share in the rewards, recognition, and benefits of all our accomplishments.

Second, simply *because you can*. When you do your job as well as it can be done you will have the personal satisfaction of knowing that you did your best.

Do your part. Take pride in knowing that you are part of a team that is committed to achieving an extraordinary goal—*World-Class Service*.

It is easy, actually, to
"exceed the expectations"
of most customers.

Just be polite and nice to them
and give them what they want
the way they want it
when they want it.

This will exceed their
expectations because
they won't expect it.

—Jim Ball

Seven Steps to Service They'll Remember

THERE ARE SEVEN STEPS to providing memorable service. They are listed below and explained on the following pages.

When you do your part in applying these seven steps, we will be able to meet our goal of providing *World-Class Service*.

Step 1: Adopt a Service Mentality

Step 2: Adopt a World-Class Approach

Step 3: Be Fun to Do Business With

Step 4: Think Speed and Accuracy

Step 5: Do Something Extra

Step 6: Improve Continually

Step 7: Use a Total Team Approach

Step 1:
Adopt a Service Mentality

THE FIRST STEP toward *World-Class Service* is for everyone in our company to adopt a service mentality.

This means that we all keep ever-present in mind the reason our business exists. Customers are the reason. Without our customers none of us would have jobs here.

When our customers call us or visit our facilities, they are our guests. We must go out of our way to serve them and make them glad they contacted us.

✴ We should always be courteous and respectful when speaking with our customers.

✴ We should thank our customers for their business. We should never take them for granted.

Finally, we constantly should be on the lookout for ways to serve our customers better and faster.

Dos and Don'ts

Do:

- Remember that our customers are the reason our business exists.

- Speak, think, and act positively about our customers.

- Appreciate our customers.

- Look for ways to be helpful to them.

- Provide the best service you can provide.

- Say "thank you" when customers provide us business or give us an opportunity to serve them.

Don't:

- Underestimate the importance of your part in creating and promoting a customer service mentality in our company. What you say and do can and will make a difference.

- Speak or act negatively to or about our customers.

- Ignore our customers.

The Extraordinary Seamstress

IT WAS THE THURSDAY before the wedding when a friend called and asked if I knew of a seamstress who could do an emergency complex hem job on her mother-of-the-bride dress.

I called a seamstress someone had told me about and asked if she could hem the dress on such short notice. Without hesitation, complaint, or disgruntlement the woman said: "Yes, I think so. Could you bring the dress to my shop this evening?"

When I dropped the dress off at 9:00 p.m. that evening the polite seamstress thanked me for the work and said it would be ready the next morning. Morning arrived and the dress was perfectly hemmed, pressed, and ready at 8:00 a.m.

I thanked the seamstress over and over when I picked the dress up and again the following Tuesday when I went back with gifts of fresh flowers and a small box of chocolates.

She cried when I handed her the flowers.

I don't think anyone had ever shown her how much they appreciated her and her work. I was so glad I had taken the few minutes to pick up two simple gifts and go back to thank her in person. I think I made her day. I know she made mine.

—Jennifer

Service to others is the best
work of life.

—Various authors

Step 2:
Adopt a World-Class Approach

THE SECOND STEP toward *World-Class Service* is for everyone in our company to think and act in a world-class manner.

If we are going to provide *World-Class Service*, we must be the best. Period.

We must look at every detail and every aspect of what we do, and make it the best possible.

We cannot tolerate mediocrity or be satisfied with anything less than the best that we can provide.

Dos and Don'ts

Do:

- Act in a world-class manner.
- Be world-class in spirit.
- Set a world-class example for others to follow.
- Take steps to improve the quality of our products and services—raise the bar.
- Find ways to become the best at what you do.

Don't:

- Settle for mediocrity.
- Cut corners.

Presentation with Flair

HAVE YOU ever known the minute you walked into a little shop that there was something special about it?

The first time I visited a florist near our office all I wanted was a single stem for a bud vase on my desk. The woman behind the counter helped me select a beautiful orange gerbera daisy.

You should have seen the care she took to wrap my daisy for me. First, she wrapped a fine wire around the stem to support it. Next, she slipped the end into a plastic vial of water. Then, she added a sprig of greenery and wrapped the flower in clear plastic. Finally, she tied the plastic wrap with raffia and placed a gold seal on the outside.

When the woman was finished, she handed me my treasure and said, "That will be two-fifty, plus tax."

Isn't that amazing? A simple flower became a beautiful work of art and the price was just two dollars and fifty cents.

I have been back many times and I've never been disappointed. In fact, I'm always simply delighted. Whether it is a substantial arrangement or a simple two-dollar stem, my favorite florist takes a world-class approach to every order they fill.

—Jennifer

*If you are going to forget the
details, you might as well just
forget it altogether.*

—Jennifer Kuchta

Step 3:
Be Fun to Do Business With

THE THIRD STEP toward *World-Class Service* is to be fun to do business with.

Everyone would rather do business with happy, friendly people who enjoy their jobs and are having fun doing them.

You can make your job fun and enjoyable or you can make it tedious and boring. It all begins with you and your attitude.

If you are having fun and if you are fun to be around, you will attract customers. They will enjoy doing business with you.

No one likes a grouch. No one wants to deal with a scrooge, or a crank.

This does not suggest that you should be frivolous. Our company depends on mature individuals. But our mature individuals always strive to be pleasant.

Dos and Don'ts

Do:

- Smile. Smile. Smile.
- Adopt a positive attitude.
- Have fun and enjoy your work.
- Learn to laugh at yourself.
- Keep your sense of humor.
- Bring out the best in others.
- Look for ways to make your work more enjoyable and fun.

Don't:

- Be a grouch.
- Take things too seriously.
- Get silly or nonsensical.
- Act in an immature manner.
- Play practical jokes.
- Just put in time.

My Friend at the Cleaners

I DRIVE TEN MILES out of my way, sometimes through thick traffic, to a dry cleaning shop that is located near my previous office.

It is not convenient, but I have been going to this same shop for fifteen years. I'll continue going there as long as the woman who waits on me works there.

When she sees me enter the door she lights up. "Hello!" she greets me. "How good to see you again!"

I feel like I have just gone for a visit with a good friend. And, as I have thought about this over the years, I have realized that is exactly what I am doing.

It takes only a minute to drop off my clothes or pick them up. But in that short time, my friend at the cleaners makes me feel good and glad that I am alive.

It's her instant excitement in seeing me. Her broad smile and joy in asking me how I've been. Her special "Thank you! Hope to see you soon." Small things really. But done so sincerely, and with such enthusiasm.

She starts my day off on such a high note I couldn't imagine going anywhere else.

—Jim

If you forgot your smile today,
I'll give you mine.

—Greeting on a
salesclerk's badge

Step 4:
Think Speed and Accuracy

THE FOURTH STEP toward *World-Class Service* is to think speed and accuracy.

Speed and accuracy are important because our customers value their time. They want to complete their purchases as fast as possible.

Our customers want to be served promptly. When they are ready to be helped, they want to be helped immediately. They do not want to stand in line waiting to place their order. They do not want delivery of their goods and services to take forever. They want them now.

Our job is to serve them now—no waiting in line, no holding on the telephone, no waiting for delivery.

Our customers also want accuracy. They do not want us to make mistakes.

Our job is to serve them correctly without errors.

Yes, it puts pressure on us to serve our customers quickly and accurately. But this is our challenge. We can do it.

When we respond faster than our competitors, we will win more business than our competitors.

If we respond slower than our competitors, we will see our business slip away.

Dos and Don'ts

Do:

- Think speed and accuracy.
- Move quickly when serving our customers.
- Step back from your work and evaluate how you can do it better and quicker.
- Set the pace for others to follow.
- Encourage others to pick up the pace.
- Get it right the first time.
- Check your work for accuracy.

Don't:

- Move in a slow or sluggish manner.
- Take more time than necessary to complete a task.
- Distract others or slow them down.
- Make careless errors.

"I Promise"

I FOUND THE EXACT WATCH I was looking for as a gift for my wife's birthday.

"That's one of my favorites," the woman behind the counter said. "May I gift wrap it for you?"

Before I could answer, she added, "It won't take a minute, I promise."

It was her 'I promise' that got me. I believed her. So, even though I was in a hurry, I decided to have her wrap my present.

She was indeed very fast. In almost no time she had my gift beautifully wrapped and tied with a bow.

It amazed me that in that short amount of time I found another item that I decided to purchase. She wrapped that one too, in about a minute, just like she promised.

What a huge difference those two little words made: "I promise."

—*Jim*

*The speed of your service will
improve the more often you get
it right the first time.*

—Jim Ball

Step 5:
Do Something Extra

THE FIFTH STEP toward *World-Class Service* is to do something extra.

If we do only what our customers expect, we will never be able to set our company apart from the pack and become world-class.

When we are world-class, we do what everyone else does as well as they do it, *and more*.

We must do something extra and we must do it continually and repeatedly. When we do something extra we provide our customers with some thing or some service that they did not ask for or expect. It might be the quantity, or the quality, or the timing, or the style— something extra.

This book is not trying to tell you all the examples of all the types of extras you can give to our customers. It is trying to show you that we need help identifying and providing those special extras.

Sometimes we find a large or unusual extra to perform. But usually, it is the *little* extras that add up: the multitude of little details, such as remembering a customer's name, and having an extra warm and friendly smile.

Dos and Don'ts

Do:

- Think "extra." What can you do extra for our customers?
- Take the extra steps. Go out of your way and be helpful in an extraordinary way.
- Make our customers' day.

Don't:

- Do only what is asked of you.

Bob at the Checkout

WHEN I VISIT my neighborhood grocery store, I always head for Bob's checkout line.

Bob is having fun and he's genuinely glad to see the customers in his line. Bob doesn't just say "Hello." He says, "Hey, how's it going?" Then he continues a little conversation while he rapidly rings up my purchases.

When I'm leaving, Bob might say something like, "Thanks, Miss Kuchta. Hope you enjoy those ribs on the barbeque."

Almost every time, Bob gives me some kind of little "extra." Once he gave me a quick tip for roasting my corn on the grill. Several times he's given me one of those tootsie pop suckers that are usually just for the kids. I think Bob's extras are his way of saying, "Thanks for talking with me and caring about me, too."

I do care about Bob. He's world-class and he certainly makes a difference in my shopping experience.

—Jennifer

*The difference between ordinary
and extraordinary is that little
"extra."*

—Author unknown

Step 6:
Improve Continually

THE SIXTH STEP toward *World-Class Service* is to improve continually.

We must continually and constantly improve every aspect of our services, along with the quality, packaging, and delivery of the goods and services that we provide.

We must never become satisfied or stagnate.

Continual improvement is everyone's job. No one person or group is responsible for upgrading what we do or identifying opportunities. Each of us must be constantly on the lookout for ideas and opportunities for innovation.

Dos and Don'ts

Do:

- Be constantly on the lookout for ways to improve what you and others are doing.
- Look for ways to improve the quality of our goods and services.
- Pay attention to the details.

Don't:

- Become satisfied or stagnate.
- Overlook any detail.

How the Best Get Better

EVERY MORNING at the Tower Club, a posh dining club in McLean, Virginia, the club's manager, John Nicholas, leads the "daily line up" operations meeting.

When he is nearly finished with his meeting, Nicholas opens the little 5 x 7 inch book he carries, and does what his staff reverently refers to as 'a reading from the book of John.'

Nicholas is not reading from the Bible; it's *Professionalism Is for Everyone,* another book in the *Keep It Simple for Success* series.

"We are always looking for something to refresh our enthusiasm for perfection," Nicholas says. "This little book is perfect. It helps me build rapport with my staff and it provides a daily forum to reinforce our culture and our continual quest for improvement. With the book I can discuss positive values and important issues that are sometimes difficult to bring up without sounding like I'm preaching—no pun intended."

"What I like best," says Constance Gleeson, a lead server at the club, "is that the book is inspiring. We all want to do our best and John's readings are so energizing."

—Jim

Good enough never is.

—Author unknown

Step 7:
Use a Total Team Approach

THE SEVENTH STEP toward *World-Class Service* is to use a total team approach.

Although we each must do our part in serving our customers, none of us can do it alone. Together, we are better than any one of us is by himself or herself.

We must take time to evaluate our team approach. Then we must continually look for ways to work better, smarter, and faster together.

This means more coordination, clearer communication, and practice. We have to practice as a team if we are going to serve as a team.

As team members, we each must help other team members learn their roles and tasks so they can develop and grow. If we encourage each other in our team efforts, we will be able to take pride in our team results.

Dos and Don'ts

Do:

- Think and act as a team member.
- Get to know your team members.
- Take steps to improve your team's performance and results in serving our customers.
- Help your team members develop and grow.
- Encourage team members.
- Seek help and advice when you need it.

Don't:

- Try to do it all yourself.
- Be a slacker.
- Nag, complain, or discourage.
- Blame others.

Our Favorite Restaurant

MY FAMILY and I have been going to the same local Italian restaurant once or twice a month *for more than twenty-five years*.

The food is excellent and the white tablecloths and tuxedoed-waiter ambiance are special as well.

What we love most is the personalized care and attention that we receive from everyone.

We love it when the maitre d' beams when we arrive and goes out of his way to greet us.

We love it when, without our asking, our favorite waiter appears with our favorite wine.

We love it when the chef prepares a dish we like that is not on the menu.

We love it when the owner sends complimentary dessert to our table as a surprise gift "on the house."

Now that our daughters are young adults, they go to this restaurant with their friends, as well. We had the reception for our older daughter's wedding there.

While each individual at our favorite restaurant is great, as a team they are truly superb. That is why we keep going back.

—Jim

*Teamwork is not
work done by teams.*

It is people working together.

—Jim Ball

Our Customers *Are* Our Business

"If we do not love our customers,
then someone else will."

WHOEVER COINED this little phrase captured the essence of what every successful business is all about.

The purpose of our business is to find, serve, satisfy, and keep our customers.

And what better way is there to satisfy and keep our customers than to love serving them and pleasing them?

Think about that for a moment.

Through the dollars they spend with us, our customers provide the fuel that runs our company.

When we care about our customers and satisfy them, they enjoy doing business with us, and our business prospers. We can then provide opportunities for career growth and development.

If we do not enjoy serving our customers, they soon will prefer doing business with a competitor who does. We will lose our customers. They will spend their money where they are appreciated. This will reduce our resources and the opportunities we are able to provide.

The challenges we face

Serving customers is seldom easy. At times it is downright challenging—particularly for those of us who are on the front lines of customer service.

The individuals who wait on our customers, answer their questions, and listen to and respond to their complaints are in some of the most difficult and demanding positions in our company.

It takes special efforts and skills to please our customers when they are not being easy to please.

Easy or not, we need your help in satisfying our customers' needs and wants so that they return to do business with us again and again and again.

Customer Bill of Rights

When you stop to think about it, our customers have the right to expect many things of us.

Just think about how you feel when you make a purchase. Think about what you should expect when you give a business an opportunity to serve you.

You have many rights as a customer. Our customers have these same rights. We have summarized these rights as the *Customer Bill of Rights* and explained them more fully in the pages that follow.

When all is said and done,
we will be judged,
not by the customers we get,
but by those that we keep.

—Author unknown

World-Class Customer Service:

Customer Bill of Rights

OUR CUSTOMERS have the following inalienable rights:

1. Honesty and Truthfulness
2. Friendly Service with a Smile
3. Appreciation
4. Courtesy and Respect
5. Individual Attention
6. Fair and Full Value
7. Satisfaction Guaranteed
8. Professional Service
9. A Safe and Clean Environment
10. Fast, Easy, and Hassle-Free Service

1. Honesty and Truthfulness

OUR CUSTOMERS HAVE THE RIGHT to honesty and truthfulness.

- They have the right to be told the truth, the whole truth, and nothing but the truth.

- They have the right to expect that they will not be mislead in any way.

- They have the right to be informed immediately of the status of their order and any problems or delays.

Dos and Don'ts

Do:

- Tell our customers the truth, the whole truth, and nothing but the truth.

- Describe our products and services factually, correctly, and properly.

- Keep our customers truthfully informed and up to date about the status of their orders.

Don't:

- Mislead our customers in any way.

- Overstate or exaggerate.

2. Friendly Service with a Smile

OUR CUSTOMERS HAVE THE RIGHT to friendly service with a smile.

- They have the right to be waited on by someone who is happy to be waiting on them.

- They have the right to be served by someone who looks them in the eye and gives them a warm and sincere smile.

- They have the right to expect whoever is helping them to be enthusiastic and energetic.

Dos and Don'ts

Do:

- Smile when you greet our customers.
- Be happy and friendly.
- Be energetic and enthusiastic.
- Look our customers in the eye.

Don't:

- Be rude.
- Be grumpy.
- Act like you are tired or bored.

3. Appreciation

OUR CUSTOMERS HAVE THE RIGHT to appreciation.

- They have the right to be appreciated for their business.

- They have the right to expect us to show and express our appreciation.

Dos and Don'ts

Do:

- Be thankful for the opportunities our customers provide us to serve them.
- Say "Thank you for your business!"

Don't:

- Take our customers for granted.
- Be insincere.
- Treat our customers as though they are interrupting your work.

4. Courtesy and Respect

OUR CUSTOMERS HAVE THE RIGHT to courtesy and respect.

- They have the right to be treated as guests.
- They have the right to be acknowledged immediately when they enter our facilities or contact us.
- They have the right to be shown proper manners and polite, proper conversation.
- They have the right to attentive service.

Dos and Don'ts

Do:

- Treat our customers as guests in every way.
- Acknowledge our customers immediately when they enter our business or contact us.
- Say "please" and "thank you."
- Use proper manners and polite and proper conversation.
- Be fully attentive when serving our customers.

Don't:

- Do something else, like talk on the telephone or visit with a friend, when serving our customers.
- Use foul or improper language.
- Ignore or avoid our customers.
- Act superior to our customers.
- Argue with our customers.
- Embarrass our customers.
- Insult our customers or be rude in any way.

5. Individual Attention

OUR CUSTOMERS HAVE THE RIGHT to individual attention.

- They have the right to be called by name when it is possible to do so.

- They have the right to purchase our products and services in a manner that meets their individual needs and personal preferences.

- They have the right to be treated as unique individuals—real live human beings—not as numbers or impersonal objects.

Dos and Don'ts

Do:

● Use "Sir" or "Madam" when addressing customers that you do not know by name.

● Refer to our customers as "Mr." or "Ms." and use their last names when you know them.

● Seek immediate help from others if you encounter questions or issues you cannot resolve.

● Be receptive and helpful in providing individualized service.

● Let customers tailor our goods and services to their preferences if it is reasonably possible to do so and consistent with our company's policies.

Don't:

● Give our customers a hard time.

● Treat our customers as numbers or impersonal objects.

6. Fair and Full Value

OUR CUSTOMERS HAVE THE RIGHT to fair and full value.

- They have the right to get the proper quantity and value of the goods and services they purchased.

- They have the right to a fair and reasonable price for our goods and services.

- They have the right to all available discounts, premiums, and options.

Dos and Don'ts

Do:

* Do what is fair and reasonable at all times.

* Provide the quantity and quality of goods and services our customers expect to acquire.

* Provide the best price available, including all available discounts, premiums, and options.

Don't:

* Shortchange our customers in price, quantity, quality, or service.

* Take advantage of our customers.

7. Satisfaction Guaranteed

OUR CUSTOMERS HAVE THE RIGHT to satisfaction guaranteed.

- They have the right to complete and reasonable satisfaction with our goods and services.
- They have the right to a full and prompt refund or an exchange for comparable products or services at comparable prices.

Dos and Don'ts

Do:

- Make sure that our customers are satisfied with their purchases.

- Provide appropriate refunds, exchanges, or accommodations to customers. Always follow our company policies and procedures for adjusting errors, irregularities, or problems.

- Apologize to our customers for any errors, irregularities, or mistakes we may have made.

- Seek assistance from a supervisor if you feel a customer is making demands and claims that are significantly out of line or inappropriate.

Don't:

- Challenge our customers or argue with them.

- Make it difficult for our customers to express a complaint, get a refund or exchange, or have a dissatisfaction resolved in a reasonable manner.

- Try to prove our customers wrong.

8. Professional Service

OUR CUSTOMERS HAVE THE RIGHT to professional service.

- They have the right to be waited on by someone who is properly trained and has good knowledge of our products and services.

- They have the right to be served by someone who is capable.

- They have the right to be served competently, quickly, and accurately.

- They have the right to expect our associates to present a professional image, communicate well, and be fully attentive, polite, courteous, and respectful.

Dos and Don'ts

Do:

- Learn your job and acquire the training and skills you need to do it properly and professionally.

- Perform as well as you possibly can.

- Maintain a professional image by paying attention to your appearance and grooming.

- Be prompt, timely, responsible, and attentive.

- Follow through on your promises and commitments.

Don't:

- Dress sloppily or become careless with your appearance or grooming.

- Act unprofessionally.

- Be lackadaisical, casual, or improper.

9. A Safe and Clean Environment

OUR CUSTOMERS HAVE THE RIGHT to a safe and clean environment.

- They have the right to clean and properly functioning facilities including our restrooms.

- They have the right to well-lighted facilities that are free of odors and hazards, and hazardous or toxic materials.

- They have the right to expect security and safety while in our facilities.

Dos and Don'ts

Do:

- Help keep the inside and outside of our facilities, including our restrooms, clean, well-lighted, and free of debris and clutter.
- Clean up after yourself—at your desk, in the lunchroom, and elsewhere.
- Put things away in their proper place.
- Pick up trash when you see it on the floor.
- Report to your supervisor immediately any hazardous or unsafe condition.

Don't:

- Expect someone else to clean up after you.
- Allow an unsafe or hazardous condition to exist.

10. Fast, Easy, and Hassle-Free Service

OUR CUSTOMERS HAVE THE RIGHT to fast, easy, and hassle-free service.

- They have the right to be waited on promptly and properly.

- They have the right to a straightforward and simple transaction when buying from us.

- They have the right to receive their goods and services on time.

- They have the right to expect it to be easy and problem-free to do business with us.

Dos and Don'ts

Do:

- Wait on our customers promptly and as fast as you reasonably can.

- Make it as easy and problem-free as you can for our customers to do business with us.

- Be helpful and offer assistance when you sense it is needed.

- Keep it simple.

Don't:

- Overexplain.

- Require more steps, forms, or actions of a customer than are necessary.

- Hassle our customers in any way.

- Pester or insist on helping a customer who seems to want to be left alone.

*Your customers are not an
interruption of your work.
Rather, they are the reason that
you have work.*

—Jim Ball

It's Up to You!

THIS BOOK IS ABOUT TO END. But your thoughts and the actions inspired by this book are just beginning.

You Make a Difference!

Reflect on the fact that you make a difference in the service we provide and in the customers we retain.

This is worth repeating. Not only do you make a difference, we *need* you to make that difference. We are counting on you to do it.

World-Class Service and You

Our goal is providing *World-Class Service*.

This is a big goal.

But this is the only goal that makes sense if we are going to be a successful company. To do that, we must be the best.

We need your help to achieve our goal.

You are on the team. Pitch in and make a difference.

Seven Steps to Service They'll Remember

In this book, we described seven steps for providing *World-Class Service*.

We need your help in implementing each of these: Adopting a service mentality, adopting a world-class approach, being fun to do business with, thinking speed and accuracy, doing something extra, improving continually, and using a total team approach.

When you implement each of these steps, you will provide service our customers will truly remember.

And they will remember you, too!

Our Customers *Are* Our Business

The most important business reality in this book is that our business exists for only one reason.

It is to find, serve, satisfy, and keep our customers.

Customer Bill of Rights

In return for their patronage, we acknowledge ten inalienable rights of our customers: Honesty and truthfulness, friendly service with a smile, appreciation, courtesy and respect, individual attention, fair and full value, satisfaction guaranteed, professional service, a safe and clean environment, and fast, easy, and hassle-free service.

The way to provide these rights on a consistent and reliable basis is to treat our customers as true guests. If we do not treat our customers as they want to be treated, someone else will.

So, when you greet our customers, remember that they are our guests. Give them their rights and show them that you care.

Now, It's Up to You

We hope you are inspired and motivated to act.

When you do, your rewards will be great. You will like the person you will become, the respect you will enjoy, and the self-esteem and self-confidence that come only from being the very, very best that you can be.

Many wise men and women have said that service to humanity is the best work of life.

And, where is a better place to begin than with our customers? And, when is a better time to begin than now? And, who would be better to begin than you?

Best wishes for great success, tremendous happiness, and *World-Class Service.*

You really do make a difference!

World-Class Customer Service:

About the Authors

JAMES R. BALL is CEO and JENNIFER A. KUCHTA is Vice President and Publisher of The Goals Institute, the company they founded to help businesses and organizations achieve their potential through goal achievement.

Mr. Ball and Ms. Kuchta provide keynotes and leadership seminars for businesses and associations.

James R. Ball

Jim Ball was the co-founder and CEO of Venture America, a venture capital firm that helped launch over twenty companies, including The Discovery Channel.

Before that, he was a managing partner at Arthur Andersen. He has been an adjunct faculty member at George Mason University where he co-founded George Mason University Entrepreneurial Institute, Inc.

Mr. Ball is a certified public accountant and member of the American Institute of Certified Public Accountants. He and his wife Dolly live in Virginia. They have two daughters, Jennifer and Stephanie.

Jennifer A. Kuchta

Jennifer Kuchta oversaw finance, administration, investor relations, and services and support of portfolio companies at Venture America.

Before that, Ms. Kuchta was a marketing support specialist for field sales representatives of fine arts. She has a degree in accounting and is a member of many business and civic organizations.

Other books by James R. Ball

The *Keep It Simple for Success*™ series:

> *ABCs for Life:*
> *26 Principles for Success and Happiness*
>
> *Professionalism Is for Everyone:*
> *Five Keys to Being a True Professional*

Additional books:

> *Soar . . . If You Dare*®
>
> *DNA Leadership through Goal-Driven*
> *Management*
>
> *The Entrepreneur's Tool Kit*

World-Class Customer Service:

*Our customers want us to have
many abilities. The one that they
most want us to have is
reliability.*

—Jim Ball

Best wishes for
great success and happiness!

IF YOU WOULD LIKE more information about our other *Keep It Simple for Success* titles, discounts for volume purchases, or our speaking and leadership seminar services, or would like to send us your comments or suggestions, please contact or visit us at:

The Goals Institute
P.O. Box 3736
Reston, VA 20195-1736
703·264·2000

www.goalsinstitute.com
www.kissbooks.com
Email: info@goalsinstitute.com